FEAR NOT

Two Weeks of Living Boldly into
God's Authentic Confidence

JOHN KAITES

WESTBOW
PRESS®
A DIVISION OF THOMAS NELSON
& ZONDERVAN

WestBow Press books may be ordered through booksellers or by contacting:

WestBow Press
A Division of Thomas Nelson & Zondervan
1663 Liberty Drive
Bloomington, IN 47403
www.westbowpress.com
1 (866) 928-1240

ISBN: 978-1-5127-8143-4 (sc)
ISBN: 978-1-5127-8145-8 (hc)
ISBN: 978-1-5127-8144-1 (e)

Library of Congress Control Number: 2017904920

Print information available on the last page.

WestBow Press rev. date: 06/07/2017

Contents

How to Use This Book

This book is audacious enough to dare you to live fearlessly—to rest completely in God's love and to let that perfect love drive out your fears. The goal of this book is more than to inform you; it is to transform you.

This book recognizes that transformation is nearly always gradual. True transformation takes time, effort, and persistence. Transformation does not happen immediately. This is why this book has a devotional structure: There are fourteen chapters for two weeks of thinking about fearlessness. The two weeks have slightly different focuses. Week 1 investigates the foundation of a fearless life: What instructions does the Bible give us, and how do they combine to form the elements of fearlessness? Week 2 examines the tools in a fearless Christian's toolbox: What does it look like to live out our God-given fearlessness? How does God equip us to do so faithfully? The two weeks combine to illustrate the fearless Christian life and show you that you can live fearlessly and boldly, rooted in the love of God.

Take your time. Read one section per day and let those thoughts linger in your mind and transform your thoughts and actions for that day. By the end of two weeks, you will not have perfected living fearlessly, but I hope that you will have developed some of the habits that will guide you more and more into a daring fearlessness.

This book suggests a small action you can take each day to draw closer to the fearless life to which God calls you. You can read this devotional at whatever time fits your schedule, but I recommend that you revisit the "Action" section as you start your day. Let these actions serve as a theme to your day, and let them help you put ideas into practice as you begin to be transformed by your progress into fearlessness.

Endnotes are provided in this book if you want to dig deeper. These sources will allow readers to investigate where these thoughts are coming from and the context from which these ideas have grown in my mind. Use them if they are helpful, but feel free to skip them if they are distracting.

May the Lord miraculously bless you through His words and through the words in this book. In the name of His Son Jesus Christ, amen!

Week 1

Living a Life without Fear

Have you ever thought that you could live a life free of fear? Most people believe that fear is something that we all have to live with and that we can work around or fight through fear. Fear is something that we can eliminate from our daily lives. The insecurities and negative, fear-based thoughts that every human has really can be minimized—and even eliminated. God gives us a pathway toward that goal.

In this first week, we will look at what it means to live in God's reality from a heart grounded in love rather than in fear. Before we discuss how to become fearless, let us examine why it is worth your time to do so. Living fearlessly will allow you to live a life with God's authentic confidence, to solve problems more easily, to deal with pain and mistakes better, to be more creative and more loving, and to enrich all your personal relationships. It will allow you to appreciate all that you have and to live a life full of joy and devoid of fear.

On March 4, 1933, a newly elected Franklin D. Roosevelt delivered his first inaugural address. In the address, Roosevelt remarked memorably that "the only thing we have to fear is fear itself—nameless, unreasoning, unjustified terror which paralyzes needed efforts to convert retreat into advance."[1]

We see these words quoted often, but we don't often think of the context in which Roosevelt was speaking. The new president was addressing a country that had been hit hard by the Great Depression. Roosevelt addressed the country with the knowledge that fear is a force that can take over a person's mind and the mind of a nation. Fear leads us from thoughtful action to impulsive reaction, and a fearful response nearly always makes the situation worse. Roosevelt opened his inaugural address by encouraging people to turn from fear because fear is ultimately only a destructive force—one which restrains us from achieving our potential.

Maybe Roosevelt knew that a reaction to a fear-based emotion is almost always going to lead to the wrong outcome, but that one made out of love will almost always lead to the right outcome. If we fear these outcomes, we're going to lose against them. If we live in fear, we won't be able to beat these outcomes.

Fear-based responses generally produce only negative results. Shortly after the sinking of the *Titanic*, the *Eastland* sank, and it had more casualties than the *Titanic*. The general opinion of historians is that the *Eastland* sank because it had *more* lifeboats on it than the ship could handle. The ship sank so quickly from the unbalanced weight that none of the lifeboats were deployed.[2] The months following the terrorist attacks of September 11, 2001, saw a sharp increase in road deaths because Americans became fearful of flying in airplanes.[3] When ruled by fear, we do not make wise choices, and choices made from fear are not guaranteed to be any safer.

In New Testament Greek, the word that we translate to mean *joy* can also be understood by translators as the absence of fear.[4] James opens his letter to God's people by urging them to rejoice when they face challenges—this opening can be understood as an admonishment to be fearless when you face challenges in your life. James goes on to write that, instead of giving in to fear, we should face our challenges in joy—or fearlessness. Through faith, we can ask God for His wisdom, and with God, we will get through it all stronger, better, and happier.

The high-level functioning of our brains is based on subconscious processes of which we are generally not aware. At the base of these processes, we find that there are two emotions that can be understood as the roots of all of our thoughts, actions, and decisions. These two emotions are love and fear. This week we will look what that means. We will begin to understand why we can and must act from love rather than from fear. A love-based response to our situations will truly allow us to live in freedom and in alignment with God. This week we will begin our journey of transformation by examining the foundational elements of living by faith rather than fear.

Day 1

Simple but Not Easy

Dear brothers and sisters, when troubles of any kind come your way, consider it an opportunity for great joy. For you know that when your faith is tested, your endurance has a chance to grow. So let it grow, for when your endurance is fully developed, you will be perfect and complete, needing nothing.

If you need wisdom, ask our generous God, and he will give it to you. He will not rebuke you for asking. But when you ask him, be sure that your faith is in God alone. Do not waver, for a person with divided loyalty is as unsettled as a wave of the sea that is blown and tossed by the wind. Such people should not expect to receive anything from the Lord.

—James 1:2–7

The General Epistle of James functions like an executive summary for the Christian walk: James gives us a map showing us to how to live by God's path. The beginning of the book is bold—James challenges us to consider all things to be joyful, even in the midst of all of life's difficulties. But that bold challenge is not without an even bolder promise: If you ask God for His wisdom, He will give it to you if you ask in total faith. Emboldened by James 1, we can confidently pray, "Lord, give us your wisdom."

There are four main themes in the Bible that speak directly of how we should live. No matter how seemingly unrelated to these central themes, every story, character, and circumstance in the Bible eventually concludes in accordance with one of these four main themes. These four themes are the following.

1.   How do we receive salvation?
2.   Our God-given job is to love God and love others.
3.   Surrender to God, and provide service to others.
4.   Fear not!

The last item—living without fear—can come only as a result of patiently, with God's help, attending to the other three items. A life lived fearlessly is one that flows out of a life lived for God.

"Fear not" is undoubtedly the most common command in the Bible. It is reiterated as many as three hundred and sixty-five times throughout the sixty-six books. In *Facing the Future without Fear*, Lloyd Ogilvie comments that there are three hundred and sixty-six "fear nots" in the Bible, one for every day of the year, including leap year.[5] God doesn't want us to go a single day without hearing His words of comfort or without being reminded that we have nothing to fear.

Living a life by God's path is simple to understand but not easy to do. But like any muscle in our bodies, the practice gets easier as we exercise the ability. The more we practice these simple principles that God has given us, the easier it is for us to perform them.

Think today about what your life would look like if truly lived with God's authentic confidence rather than with fears and insecurities. What would your relationships look like if you weren't afraid of what people thought of you? What would your career look like if you were not afraid to take risks? What would your everyday life, lived out in service to God, look like if you followed all God's directions fearlessly, not second-guessing or doubting yourself? Find one small way today in which you can trust God instead of choosing fear. And today, as you think about these things, get ready for your life to transform. Get ready for a life without fear, insecurity, guilt, anger, resentment, regret, or revenge. Fear not!

God, we thank you because you call us to follow fearlessly, surrendering to your perfect plan. Today and through the rest of my life, help me follow the simple but difficult practice of living fearlessly. Lord, give me your wisdom and favor. I pray that you be with me as I follow you fearlessly into the beautiful promises you have for me and for my role in your creation. Amen.

Day 2

Fearlessness Is Possible

With the Lord's authority I say this: Live no longer as the Gentiles do, for they are hopelessly confused. Their minds are full of darkness; they wander far from the life God gives because they have closed their minds and hardened their hearts against him. They have no sense of shame. They live for lustful pleasure and eagerly practice every kind of impurity.

But that isn't what you learned about Christ. Since you have heard about Jesus and have learned the truth that comes from him, throw off your old sinful nature and your former way of life, which is corrupted by lust and deception. Instead, let the Spirit renew your thoughts and attitudes. Put on your new nature, created to be like God—truly righteous and holy.

—Ephesians 4:17–24

Let's take a look at how your brain really works. Fear is a part of your brain's functioning, as is the ability to be fearless. We can understand some spiritual truths through science because the way that God works is rooted deeply in the way the world works. Ultimately, science is man's attempt to understand how God makes events happen.

As Christians, we undertake scientific inquiry to understand more about how God created the world and about how He created us. One emerging field in understanding how God made us is that of neuroplasticity. Neuroplasticity is the science of the changeability of your brain.[6] God made your brain to be amazingly powerful: The human brain runs on about ten watts of power, yet if we were to use a computer to perform the same number of calculations per second, that computer would require a full gigawatt of power.[7] Your brain is made up of billions of synaptic nerves that are connections that do all the computing in the brain. These nerves combine to manage all functions in our bodies and thoughts in our heads. Of all the brain power we use, which is only a fraction of what is available, 95 percent is used at an unconscious level.[8] All the thoughts, feelings, and ideas that you experience consciously every day only account for a small portion of what is happening in your brain. There is far more brain activity happening under the surface, unnoticed. Some of the unconscious functions are obvious: You don't consciously tell your heart to pump seventy times a minute, your eyelids to blink, or your stomach to digest. However, the unconscious mind goes beyond the obvious. Everything that you perceive and encounter as you go through your day is filtered through your unconscious assumptions before you become consciously aware of the thought. Every emotional thought has millions or billions of synapses that are microscopic nerves that form with other synapses to fire a tiny electrical charge between the synapses.[9] All the thoughts that take place in our brains go through this process. Each tiny synaptic nerve has its own living identity.[10] And like other living things, a synaptic nerve naturally wants to grow and becomes resistant to change in its growth pattern.[11] This means that once you shape your synaptic nerves around certain ways of thinking, your brain will automatically return to those ways of thinking without conscious intent. If you shape your thoughts to revolve around love, this can be very good news, but if you tend towards fear, this can be destructive. The good news is that your synaptic nerves can change with practice.

On a very basic level, all our emotions are based in two primal instincts: love or fear.[12] Every emotion has its foundation in either one or the other. So the *you* that is you is made up of a constant struggle of your unconscious mind between fear and love. Those billions of synaptic nerves are forming and reforming around fear-based thoughts, such as insecurity, anger, resentment, judgment, and irritation, or they are forming and reforming around love-based thoughts like compassion, happiness, kindness, joy, and authentic confidence. Scientists used to believe that by our twenties, all those synaptic nerves were formed permanently and could not be changed, meaning that we could never defeat the fears we developed as children, only manage them.[13] However, the science of neuroplasticity has shown that those nerves are capable of disconnecting around one set of unconscious thoughts and reconnecting around another. In other words, the unconscious thoughts that you have come to accept as true are thoughts that can still change. No matter how old you are, you can change your brain.[14]

This is good news because it means that you can get rid of all the unconscious lies that cause you to believe falsely that you are not good enough—the "I'm not good enoughs" that keep us from taking on challenges that God clearly made us good enough to accomplish. The "I'm not good enoughs" that kill our dreams are all self-inflicted. But they are reversible through the mechanism called prayer that God gives us. Prayer helps us connect with a God who loves us, and in doing so, it physically rewires our brains.[15] Prayer transforms us, helping us to discount the negative unconscious thoughts that are fiercely guarded by our synaptic nerves and instead reconnect around positive, love-based thoughts that create peace, joy, and God's authentic confidence.

This is where journaling comes in handy. In *The Best in Us,* Dr. Cleve Stevens gives an illustration of how the "I'm not good enoughs" accumulate in the unconscious mind. He recommends journaling with a pen, not typing, as a means to identify and unlock self-doubt.[16] This practice can help create a ritual to transform and eliminate physically those unconscious lies that hold us back.[17] This process illustrates how your brain changes as you begin to see the world through God's authentic love.

It is tough to do any of this alone, but with a perfect third party, namely God, this transformative work really can be done! It can be done through God's authentic love.

So take the time to journal all your "I'm not good enoughs." Pray each morning and give them to God. Recognize the lies you believe as lies and then express the truth three times.

For instance, if you find yourself thinking, "I'm not lovable," write that down, labeling it as a lie, and write the truth three times: God has made you completely lovable and loves you completely.

In this process, ask God to take your "I'm not good enoughs" and replace them with His authentic love. Ask God to call you to a higher purpose and qualify you as you are called. Surrender all your junk to God and ask Him to give you His wisdom. Ask what you can do to serve Him and others.

Lord God, thank you for making our minds in such a way that, through your help, we can become fearless. Help me enter into this day and every day with a little more trust in you and a little less fear. Help me to live not from fear but from faith. Thank you for being my God, for watching over my life so I do not need to fear. Amen.

Day 3

Salvation

What shall we say about such wonderful things as these? If God is for us, who can ever be against us? Since he did not spare even his own Son but gave him up for us all, won't he also give us everything else? Who dares accuse us whom God has chosen for his own? No one— for God himself has given us right standing with himself. Who then will condemn us? No one— for Christ Jesus died for us and was raised to life for us, and he is sitting in the place of honor at God's right hand, pleading for us.

Can anything ever separate us from Christ's love? Does it mean he no longer loves us if we have trouble or calamity, or are persecuted, or hungry, or destitute, or in danger, or threatened with death? (As the Scriptures say, "For your sake we are killed every day; we are being slaughtered like sheep.") No, despite all these things, overwhelming victory is ours through Christ, who loved us.

And I am convinced that nothing can ever separate us from God's love. Neither death nor life, neither angels nor demons, neither our fears for today nor our worries about tomorrow—not even the powers of hell can separate us from God's love. No power in the sky above or in the earth below—indeed, nothing in all creation will ever be able to separate us from the love of God that is revealed in Christ Jesus our Lord.

—Romans 8:31–39

Now that we have discussed the more general psychological anatomy of a fearless life, let us look once more at the key messages in the Bible. We begin our journey to being fearless by examining salvation.

Of all the steps in this book, accepting God's salvation is the easiest action to take, yet the hardest to understand. Salvation is simple because all it takes is accepting the salvation that God offers to us and believing in Christ's atoning sacrifice.[18] When we accept salvation, we go from being curious to being convinced. Jesus told the disciples that "the way to the Father is through me."[19] The goal of salvation is to get to the Father. Our purpose is not just to live a good life on earth but to live forever with God and through Him. In this life, we will likely never fully understand what it means that Christ is the way to get to the Father, but it is made very clear to us in scripture that it is Christ who is the way.[20] He is your shepherd, your light, and your hope. He loves you so much that He humbled Himself, became flesh, and was humiliated, tortured, and crucified.[21] Christ sacrificed Himself to save you and then showed that He truly was God by rising again from the dead to be with the Father. He is with God and within us.[22] It's hard to fathom, but all we must do to receive salvation is to believe and accept Jesus Christ as the way, the truth, and the life.[23]

So here we stand, on the edge of salvation. Today people often ask if faith in Jesus is a good bet. Some people often claim that Jesus never lived, or that if He did live, He never did miracles, never was crucified, and never rose from the dead. These events are often called into question, but we need not have any doubts about them. For each of these events, there were many witnesses. Many people witnessed the miracles of Jesus. Many people witnessed His crucifixion. Many people witnessed His resurrection. None of these events happened in the company of just a few people; they were large public events, and there were witnesses who saw and wrote about them.[24]

The witnesses of the crucifixion of Jesus included the chief priests, scribes, elders, Roman soldiers, the two criminals crucified with Jesus, and crowds of bystanders, which included both His followers and people who did not know Him.

The witnesses of the resurrected Christ included Mary Magdalene, the women returning from the tomb, the disciples on the road to Emmaus, the apostles, the apostle Paul, and John while he was on Patmos.

Not only did these people write about the events of Jesus's life, death, and resurrection, but many of the key witnesses believed so thoroughly in what they had witnessed that they were willing to die for their beliefs.[25]

Stephen was stoned to death by the Jews. James was put to death by sword by King Herod. Peter was crucified upside-down. Matthew was also martyred by sword in Ethiopia. James, the brother of Jesus, was thrown from the top of the Temple in Jerusalem for refusing to deny Jesus. Bartholomew was flogged to death in Armenia. Andrew was crucified on an x-shaped cross in Greece. Thomas was stabbed with a spear in India. Mathias, who replaced Judas Iscariot, was stoned and then beheaded. Paul was tortured and then beheaded in Rome, and John was boiled in oil in Rome but was miraculously delivered from death. He was then exiled to the island of Patmos, where he wrote the Revelation of Saint John the Divine.

The fact that these witnesses chose to die rather than change their stories is a powerful testament to how firmly they believed and how important this faith was to them. Their testimonies ultimately all witnessed one truth: that Jesus Christ is Lord. If those who witnessed these miracles would rather be beheaded, crucified, stoned to death, imprisoned, or exiled, then we should have no need to doubt the truth that they observed.

Having this faith and gaining salvation through it, then, is the easiest to do but the hardest to understand. That Christ is with us, in us, around us and above us is hard for mere mortals to understand. Remember that the God of the universe is so big and surpasses all human understanding, and our minds can only comprehend small parts of the puzzle.

God surpasses all understanding—especially when you know He sent a part of Himself, His Son, to be our shepherd; to love us collectively and personally; to feel for us, to cry with us, and to carry us even when we don't believe in Him or give Him love back—or, worse, even when we deny Him, mock Him, or crucify Him. That is love!

All you have to do to receive salvation is to accept His love, which is hard to understand but easy to do.

If you have not yet accepted Christ and you want to, you can pray this prayer: Lord Jesus, thank you for loving me unconditionally. I love you back and accept you as my personal Lord and Savior. Forgive me for my sin and become the Lord of my life. In your name I pray. Amen.

If you just prayed the prayer above and believed what you prayed, you have just looked up at the sower of the seed. You have begun the process of becoming that fertile ground. You have achieved basic salvation.

So have faith and act. Surrender your life to God and serve by loving others and fearing nothing. He's got you. He loves you!

Day 4

Two Jobs on Earth

A lawyer asked Jesus a question. "Teacher, which is the most important commandment in the law of Moses?"

Jesus replied, "You must love the Lord your God with all your heart, all your soul, and all your mind.' This is the first and greatest commandment. A second is equally important: 'Love your neighbor as yourself.' The entire law and all the demands of the prophets are based on these two commandments."

Matthew 22:35–40

Remember that there are four main messages the Bible communicates over and over. We know that when we do the first three, we can participate in the reward of the fourth: a life without fear. If you have salvation, if you have surrendered to what God has in store for your life (which is always better than what you have planned), and if you do the job that God has set before you, then you have nothing to fear in life—not even death.

So every person, regardless of other vocations, has the same job in this life—really two jobs in one. There are many vocations but only two jobs. We see over and over again in scripture that the two jobs God gives us are to love God and love others.[26] Jesus said that on these two things "depend all the Law and the demands of the Prophets." Every command that God gives us in the Bible flows from either one command or the other, and the themes themselves are interconnected: To love God well extends to loving the people whom He has created, and to love people well reaches into loving their creator. This is why these two jobs ultimately combine into one job—our job on earth is to be rooted in profound love and to act out of that love.

"There are two commandments, greater than all the rest. The first is to love the Lord your God with all your heart, all your mind and all your spirit and the second that is equally important to love your neighbor as yourself."[27] How many times have we heard this verse, right from the lips of the perfect one—directly from Jesus and also from Moses in the Old Testament in Deuteronomy?[28] This concept also occurs in Leviticus.[29] It is not a suggestion or a request. It is your only job requirement on this planet. By the way, the easiest way to love others is to be happy with who you are. You say you are happy with yourself, are but do you actually feel it to the core? Often the things we can't stand about others are things we struggle with ourselves, either consciously or in our subconscious.

So let's break this down. Love God with your all. With all your heart, all your mind, all your spirit, and all your strength. That means a relationship with God. The cool thing is that He loves you with all His heart, mind, and spirit. God loves you enough to become like you, be humiliated by you, and even die for you to show you how much He loves you.[30] He did so to teach you how to love others.[31]

If you looked at life through this prism of loving God and loving others, then imagine how amazing your life would become. In case you are now fearful or insecure about the idea of loving or caring about someone you do not like, here is the good news. You only have to love them; you never have to like them. We tend to talk about love as though it is an emotion—we either feel it or we do not—but Jesus used *love* as a verb. Loving someone is not so much about feeling as about how you act. This is good news because we can't always change our feelings, but we can change how we act. We can choose to act lovingly even in situations that test our patience and forbearance. Even better, we can ask God to come alongside us and to give us His love for others. This is why it is possible to love even the people you do not like. If someone is mean or hurtful to you, acting lovingly does not mean that you are required to stick around and be hurt or abused. It is perfectly okay to stand up to abusers or leave any abuse, but the key here is to do so from a place of love, not anger. Consider praying every day for your enemies.[32] Forgive those who have wronged you[33] and accept those who just don't conform to your ways.

You don't have to like everyone, and you especially don't

have to like their conduct. This frees you from having to engage with people who may be destructive to you. In other words, stay away from those who are hurtful and negative forces in your life: those who are abusive, deceptive, addicted, or unreceptive to goodness. They are not fertile soil, and they will drag you down. Instead, pray for those negative people regularly and ask God to heal them in His supernatural way. Do not wish harm on them but love them from a distance and give the challenge of their lives to God to heal. You may find that after that person hits rock bottom, God will use you to plant the seed of redemption in that person's life.

If you need a more powerful way to express this message, you can use these words instead: faith and actions. Faith without actions is nothing.[34] To surrender and serve God is to acknowledge that He is the creator of all things, everything, the whole universe.[35] He knows how it all works together and where you fit in.[36] The cool point is that He has the capacity to run it all and still hear you, speak to you, and care for you in the deepest and most meaningful of ways.[37]

This all may seem complicated, but the simple way to do it is to remind yourself, as often as you can, of your two jobs: Love God and love others. Even when you are angry, say it to yourself and change your approach to others. Repeat these words to yourself and watch how cultivating love for God and others can transform your life. You can change the way your mind functions by praying for your enemies as much as you do for your friends, just as Jesus did.[38] The miracle you will see from this approach is that your enemies can become some of your greatest friends, allies, and even business partners. Love God, love others!

Start living out your two jobs today but start small. How are you already doing your jobs? How do you already show your love to God? How do you already show love to others? As you go about your day today, pay attention to small ways that you can live out both of these loves a little more.

Father God, you have created me and drawn me toward you into your perfect love. You have set before me specific tasks so that I can be your hands and feet, living in the world to shine your light. Work in me and be with me so that I can live in my calling, which you have placed on me. Show me the places in my life where I can increase in love and grant me the power to do so. God, be with your people and help us to love you and to love others well. Increase your love in us every day so that we may shine brightly in witness to you. Amen.

Day 5

Surrender/Love God

In Mark 4:1–20, we read a familiar story.

Once again Jesus began teaching by the lakeshore. A very large crowd soon gathered around him, so he got into a boat. Then he sat in the boat while all the people remained on the shore. He taught them by telling many stories in the form of parables, such as this one.

"Listen! A farmer went out to plant some seed. As he scattered it across his field, some of the seed fell on a footpath, and the birds came and ate it. Other seed fell on shallow soil with underlying rock. The seed sprouted quickly because the soil was shallow. But the plant soon wilted under the hot sun, and since it didn't have deep roots, it died. Other seed fell among thorns that grew up and choked out the tender plants so they produced no grain. Still other seeds fell on fertile soil, and they sprouted, grew, and produced a crop that was thirty, sixty, and even a hundred times as much as had been planted!" Then he said, "Anyone with ears to hear should listen and understand."

Later, when Jesus was alone with the twelve disciples and with the others who were gathered around, they asked him what the parables meant.

He replied, "You are permitted to understand the secret of the Kingdom of God. But I use parables for everything I say to outsiders, so that the Scriptures might be fulfilled:

'When they see what I do,
they will learn nothing.
When they hear what I say,
they will not understand.
Otherwise, they will turn to me
and be forgiven.'"

Then Jesus said to them, "If you can't understand the meaning of this parable, how will you understand all the other parables? The farmer plants seed by taking God's word to others. The seed that fell on the footpath represents those who hear the message, only to have Satan come at once and take it away. The seed on the rocky soil represents those who hear the message and

immediately receive it with joy. But since they
don't have deep roots, they don't last long. They
fall away as soon as they have problems or are
persecuted for believing God's word. The seed
that fell among the thorns represents others
who hear God's word, but all too quickly the
message is crowded out by the worries of this
life, the lure of wealth, and the desire for other
things, so no fruit is produced. And the seed
that fell on good soil represents those who hear
and accept God's word and produce a harvest of
thirty, sixty, or even a hundred times as much
as had been planted!"

The second theme of the Bible, love for God and for others, is
all about our mindset. Now we move into actions. Today and
tomorrow will focus on the third theme of the Bible, which is
surrender and service. Surrender is the practical outpouring of
our love for God. Service reflects our love for others. Together,
the two practices help us to live out our God-given jobs and to
live in God's authentic confidence.

One of Jesus's best-known parables is the story of the sower
of seed (farmer).[39] It is in three of the four gospels. What makes
it amazing is the fact that Jesus Himself explains what it means.
When Jesus said this parable to the multitudes on the banks of
Sea of Galilee, everyone must have been scratching their heads,
but later that night Jesus's disciples asked Him to explain the
story.

When we read the story, it's not hard to see why the disciples were confused when Jesus told His parable of the sower. Here are the basics that Jesus gives us for interpreting it: You are the soil. Jesus is the farmer. All of us are given seeds from Christ. Every day, every minute, and every second, our experiences in the world are seeds that we are receiving from God. We all have access to these seeds from God, and we are all given the same amount. The questions, then, are, "How open are we to these seeds?" and "How good is our soil?" Some people, no matter what happens or how God reaches out to them, reject the seeds planted by God in their life as if they have never seen God's presence in their life—as if Satan plucks the seed away before it can ever take root. Most people are shallow soil or the soil on rocky ground. They believe in a higher power, or they are spiritual, but they do little to develop the relationship or learn about the perfect one who loves them. So when their faith is challenged, they wither away. Then there are those who get the relationship with God and seek His knowledge and wisdom but get sucked back into the ways of the world. The love of money, lust, the need to be right, arrogance, pride, and other temptations act as thorns that tear us down. But the few who love God with all their heart, mind, strength, and spirit, who seek His knowledge and wisdom, who do their two jobs and surrender and serve the Lord—these are the people who are good soil and will be opened to experiences of greater joy, deeper relationships, better personal success, and even a life without fear. Jesus promises that what was sown will multiply thirty, sixty and even, best of all, a hundred times.

To become good soil is to become receptive to the word of God. We become good soil as we begin to live more and more in God's paradigm rather than our own.

We have a tendency to avoid talking about the words we don't like. *Surrender* is one of those words we don't talk about much. We often associate the idea of surrender with failure. What we fail to see is that when the one we are surrendering ourselves to is God, the surrender is not a failure but a resounding success. God wants the best for you, and surrendering to God's influence in your life will lead to a different kind of success—you will begin to grow into the person God intends you to be, and you will begin to live the life God intends you to have.

As you grow into that kind of person, you are being tilled and becoming good soil. And here's the really beautiful aspect: As we become good soil, God gives us the opportunity to turn around and become the sowers of the seed. It's freeing to be called to sow seed because the sower is not the one who is required to close the deal. Our part is to leave seeds that reflect God in others' lives and let God do the work of bringing those seeds to germination.

So what are the mechanics of surrender and service? It all starts with your two jobs: Love God. Love others. By doing these two things, you can go deeper in your relationship by learning how to listen for God's direction. We cannot serve our master without knowing what He expects of us. This brings us to wonder what it really means to hear God. It requires taking the time to look for God and to listen for Him. The story of the sower of the seed is a story that reminds us that God is giving all of us seeds—opportunities to see and hear Him. The question is, however, how fertile our soil is. In other words, God is reaching out to all of us with equal opportunity to hear His direction, feel His love, and receive His blessing. The question is: Are we listening?

Look for those seeds in you today: that nudge from the Holy Spirit, that relationship with God. Worship Him. Listen for Him in thoughts, prayers, and circumstances. Forgive others and be grateful in all things.

Today, say to God: "I love you, God. I surrender to you my life. I give all that I have to you for your purpose because I trust you above all else. I am the trustee of all that you have given me. Give me your wisdom and tell me what you want me to do, and I will do it. Give me the faith and the tools to make the improbable probable and the impossible possible because you are my Lord, my Savior and my king."

Pray that prayer every day and live it. When you do, you will notice the improbable becoming probable and the impossible becoming possible.

Day 6

Service/Love Others

As we read in Luke 10:25–37, one day an expert in religious law stood up to test Jesus by asking him this question: "Teacher, what should I do to inherit eternal life?"

Jesus replied, "What does the law of Moses say? How do you read it?"

The man answered, "'You must love the Lord your God with all your heart, all your soul, all your strength, and all your mind.' And, 'Love your neighbor as yourself.'"

"Right!" Jesus told him. "Do this and you will live!"

The man wanted to justify his actions, so he asked Jesus, "And who is my neighbor?"

Jesus replied with a story: "A Jewish man was traveling from Jerusalem down to Jericho, and

33

he was attacked by bandits. They stripped him of his clothes, beat him up, and left him half dead beside the road.

"By chance a priest came along. But when he saw the man lying there, he crossed to the other side of the road and passed him by. A Temple assistant walked over and looked at him lying there, but he also passed by on the other side.

"Then a despised Samaritan came along, and when he saw the man, he felt compassion for him. Going over to him, the Samaritan soothed his wounds with olive oil and wine and bandaged them. Then he put the man on his own donkey and took him to an inn, where he took care of him. The next day he handed the innkeeper two silver coins, telling him, 'Take care of this man. If his bill runs higher than this, I'll pay you the next time I'm here.'

"Now which of these three would you say was a neighbor to the man who was attacked by bandits?" Jesus asked.

The man replied, "The one who showed him mercy."

Then Jesus said, "Yes, now go and do the same."

The best way to love God is by loving the ones He loves, which includes everyone. Now on to the second part of your job: loving others. One of the best ways to begin to love others truly is to stop judging them. Jesus said, "Judge not lest ye be judged."[40] In other words, God will judge you the way you judge others. So unless you are perfect, stop expecting others to be perfect. Imagine what would occur if God judged us the way we judged others. We would find ourselves in deep trouble. Instead God shows us grace all the time. We never deserve it, but He still gives it because He loves us. When you approach life from a place of love, you do things that are contrary to what human nature dictates.

That brings us back to the sower of the seed. Once you become good soil, you will find that you become the farmer. You become the sower of the seed for others. So when you love others, don't be discouraged if they don't love you back. Don't be discouraged if the seeds you are planting fall on shallow soil. Our job, as we love others, is to plant the seeds and water them. It is the other person's job to be fertile soil, and the rest is up to Christ, the Son. Your job is just to be a consistent force for good in the lives of others and to leave the rest up to God. Preach the Gospels often and use words if necessary.[41] Your peace, your joy, your positive presence, your kindness, and your happiness in the face of adversity will cause others to want what you have. Then you can share how they get there—through a relationship with the creator and redeemer—Christ the Lord.

The call to serve others is a call to pay attention at times when we are drawn to focus on ourselves. Service starts from an awareness of the needs around you. How can you turn outwards today? How can you change your posture so that you are prepared to notice the needs of others? Start today by stepping outside of yourself a little bit more. Start today by observing.

Lord God, I come to you aware of how much love you have expressed for me—in the creation of the world, in beauty I witness in everyday life, and in your sacrifice for my sins on the cross. I pray, Lord, that you will draw me into a life where I can love and serve others from a place of gratitude for the way you have loved and served me. Help me to see today how I can operate from love in the decisions I make today.

Day 7

Fearless Because of His Love

Some time later, the Lord spoke to Abram in a vision and said to him, "Do not be afraid, Abram, for I will protect you, and your reward will be great."

—Genesis 15:1

So be strong and courageous! Do not be afraid and do not panic before them. For the Lord your God will personally go ahead of you. He will neither fail you nor abandon you.

—Deuteronomy 31:6

Then David continued, "Be strong and courageous, and do the work. Don't be afraid or discouraged, for the Lord God, my God, is with you. He will not fail you or forsake you.

He will see to it that all the work related to the Temple of the Lord is finished correctly.

—1 Chronicles 28:20

Say to those with fearful hearts, "Be strong, and do not fear, for your God is coming to destroy your enemies. He is coming to save you."

—Isaiah 35:4

But now, O Jacob, listen to the Lord who created you. O Israel, the one who formed you says, "Do not be afraid, for I have ransomed you. I have called you by name; you are mine.

—Isaiah 43:1

"Don't be afraid," he said, "for you are very precious to God. Peace! Be encouraged! Be strong!"

—Daniel 10:19

Don't be afraid, O land. Be glad now and rejoice, for the Lord has done great things.

—Joel 2:21

But the angel reassured them. "Don't be afraid!"
he said. "I bring you good news that will bring
great joy to all people. The Savior—yes, the
Messiah, the Lord—has been born today in
Bethlehem, the city of David!

—Luke 2:10–11

So don't be afraid, little flock. For it gives your
Father great happiness to give you the Kingdom.

—Luke 12:32

Cover to cover in the Bible, there are hundreds of times
that God tells His people not to fear or worry. However, when
we read those words, we often read this as if these are only
introductory words, easily forgotten. In reality, the repetition
of this command tells us that they are the main reward of a life
according to God's commands. This week we have discussed
the four main themes that God gives in the Bible, how they
fit together, and how they all contribute to enabling us to live
fearlessly in God's reality.

Let's begin with examining how we work as humans.
Every thought, every feeling, every emotion has its origin in
two basic emotions, love or fear.[42] Being happy, joyful, kind,
considerate, understanding, hopeful, cheerful, positive, and
caring are all expressions inspired by God's authentic love. In
a secular way, one could call it authentic confidence.[43] Being
angry, resentful, unforgiving, mean, nasty, upset, irritated, and

unhappy are all fear-based emotions. Authentic confidence contrasts with insecurity. Love contrasts with fear. Likewise, God contrasts with Satan.

God's goal for you is to love more and fear less, to become fearless because of His love.[44]

The one who is perfect is Jesus. Here is a rule of thumb: If Jesus said it, do it. If it is inconsistent with the words of Jesus, don't do it. That takes us back to loving more and fearing less. Jesus said: "Therefore I tell you, do not worry about your life … who of you by worrying can add a single hour to your life? Since you cannot do this very little thing why do you worry about the rest?"[45] Jesus wants us to trust Him more and fear less. Have faith in God more and fear less.

Imagine a whole day in your life without one fear-based thought—no insecurity about work or the kids or your spouse, no frustration that the garbage disposal won't work or the repairman just ripped you off, no anger over how others treat you, no resentment towards those who have wronged you. Imagine no self-doubt, no more "I'm not good enough, I'm not smart enough, I'm not pretty enough."[46] We think fear and insecurity are just parts of life and that they are something we just have to work around. That is a lie we have told ourselves as a "world of agreement."[47] The truth is that you can take on the challenges of life without having to worry. In fact, fear, anger, guilt, resentment, revenge, insecurity, and self-doubt actually make it harder to succeed. They physically, mentally, and emotionally get in the way of your creativity to solve problems and in the way of healthy relationships.[48] They get in the way of the authentic version of yourself.[49] They obstruct the person God made you to be.[50] Every negative decision you have ever made in your life came from your own fear or insecurity. Every good decision you have ever made in your life came from love and selflessness.

Who will you be: a person who acts out of fear or a person who acts out of God's authentic love? It is a decision you have to make now. This is not a matter you can decline to decide. When tomorrow comes, you will either encounter it with fear or live it with faith and from love. Choose today to live in love.

We all act out of both fear and love, but until we decide Jesus is right, we are destined to live a life enmeshed in conflict between our fear and His love. The amazing news is that God not only gives us the answers—He also gives us the way.[51] Buckle up. Your life is about ready to change because you can do all things through Christ who strengthens you.[52] These include including eliminating fear.

Try this today: Keep a journal or notebook by your side wherever you go. Every time you experience fear, doubt, worry, or insecurity, take a moment to write down that thought. You are telling yourself that you need to worry about these things, but that is a lie. Label that fear as a lie and write the truth about the situation three times instead. Use each of these times as a moment for a brief prayer—give your fears over to God and ask him to help you live authentically, planted firmly in faith.

Lord, thank you for showing your radical love for me—in the creation of the world, in the cross of Christ, and in the way you sustain and uphold my life every single day. Father,

John Kaites

I pray that as you continue to show your love for me, I will begin to rest more firmly in the knowledge and assurance of your love. I know that resting in your love will allow me to become fearless—and to live fearlessly a life wholly devoted to you. Amen.

Week 2

Living Fearlessly: The Tools God Gives Us to Live out His Calling

We have now looked at the elements of a fearless life. The four key themes of the Bible are elements that build on one another, leading to a life we can live fearlessly before God. For the next several days, we will examine some of the tools of this process.

The tools we will discuss this week are intentionality, prayer, love, forgiveness, and gratitude. We will then examine what it looks like to use these tools to do ministry in the midst of your everyday life. All these are tools God gives us to use so that we can be fearless like Him and sow seeds like Him. With God's help, we can grow into our fearless faith and learn to use each of these tools with results that can change the world.

Day 8

Intentionality

In Matthew 17:14–20, we read of a miraculous cure. At the foot of the mountain, a large crowd was waiting for them. A man came and knelt before Jesus and said, "Lord, have mercy on my son. He has seizures and suffers terribly. He often falls into the fire or into the water. So I brought him to your disciples, but they couldn't heal him."

Jesus said, "You faithless and corrupt people! How long must I be with you? How long must I put up with you? Bring the boy here to me." Then Jesus rebuked the demon in the boy, and it left him. From that moment the boy was well.

Afterward the disciples asked Jesus privately, "Why couldn't we cast out that demon?"

"You don't have enough faith," Jesus told them. "I tell you the truth, if you had faith even as small as a mustard seed, you could say to this mountain, 'Move from here to there,' and it would move. Nothing would be impossible."

To begin, let us examine the idea of intentionality. We must define intentionality in context with the idea of mechanism. Intentionality happens when you are truly committed to the outcome of that process. So intentionality is the unequivocal decision you make to cause a result to happen. A mechanism, by contrast, is the tool or set of tools you use to get that result.

In *The Best In Us*, Cleve Stevens writes about how he addresses the idea of intentionality and mechanism with groups he trains. Stevens presents an equation, as below.

$$\_\_\% \text{ intention} + \_\_\% \text{ mechanism} = 100\% \text{ result}$$

Stevens asks groups to arrive at a consensus on the percentage for each variable. Groups typically arrive at a consensus that between 60 and 80 percent is brought about by the intention. Stevens then delivers his answer: Results depend 100 percent on intention and 0 percent on mechanism. Stevens reflects, "A mechanism does not an intention make, but an intention always creates a mechanism for its own fulfillment. In fact, built into every true intention is the mechanism for its fulfillment."[53]

This reality is no less true when the result we are aiming for is our two jobs: loving God and loving others. When God is with us in what we intend to do, possessing the mechanism to make it happen need not concern us. There are hundreds or even thousands of ways to accomplish almost every task. We limit possibilities when we limit ourselves to acting only when we can see the whole path before us.[54] God sees all the paths and mechanisms and knows all the tools. We only know what we know. But we can know more if we are intentionally learning and seeing past the limits of our own minds. We live in what Stevens characterizes as a world of agreement: "the largely unexamined, unrecognized even, set of standards and rules that make up key elements of our culture and individual lives."[55] In this world of agreement, we all generally agree about what is possible and what is not, and we follow through by limiting our intentions and actions to outcomes that we have agreed are possible. The truth, however, is that most of the limits we place on ourselves are false. These limits are lies that we tell ourselves. We are able to do so much more.

Please reflect that up until the fifteenth century, everyone agreed the world was flat. How could it not be flat? Two hundred years ago, there was no way man could fly. Now, for the price of a ticket, you can fly anywhere you want. How about putting a man on the moon and getting him back home safely? Impossible? Yet all the mechanisms to go to the moon and back existed at the time Columbus sailed west and did not fall off the corner of the Earth or when the Wright brothers took off and flew for twenty-two minutes. Those mechanisms existed since the beginning of time. They just had not been discovered by man until we were intentional about discovering them. It was not until an entire nation's intentionality was focused on the task of putting a man on the moon that it happened.

Here's what this means for us, in our lives of following Christ and living with love for God and others. How many times have you decided not to do something good because you did not think you were good enough to get it done? God plants in all of us dreams of our possibilities, if we would only believe.[56] It is those many seeds He pours on us. When we are told by others, sometimes at a young age, that those dreams are impossible or, worse, that those dreams are not possible for us personally, our dreams die or go dormant. Consider that, except for Jesus, every other person who accomplished anything in the Bible was not qualified to do the job God gave him or her. Consider Moses, Noah, Ruth, Solomon, Esther, David, and even Jesus's disciples and the apostle Paul—there was not a single major figure in the Bible who seemed qualified, by man's standards, to do the job at hand. But because the task was good and because it served others and God wanted it done, the ones who were called and had the faith to accept the call became qualified[57] because they had faith and acted with intentionality.

God loves to surprise us with what we can accomplish. When you surrender and serve God, you will suddenly start seeing opportunities to act for good, even when you don't think you are good enough. But when you trust Him and act, He is faithful to give you the mechanisms you need to accomplish the task set before you. Often the tools don't arrive until you need them.

When God choose Moses to free the Hebrews from Egypt, Moses was not the obvious choice for leadership. In many ways, Moses was the biggest loser of his time. Once a prince of

Egypt, Moses found himself humiliated, exiled to the desert for forty years, and left to grind it out while living with sheep. Circumstances started to change for Moses, though, when God spoke to him and gave him the assignment to confront the pharaoh. Like most of us, his response was less positive than you might expect. Moses protests against the new assignment, saying, "Not me, Lord. I am a terrible speaker."

"Don't worry," God replies, "I will give you Aaron, he will help you."[58] Not only did God provide Moses with Aaron as a helper, He provided the tools that Moses needed just as he needed them. In this case, the tools came in miraculous forms: the plagues of Egypt, the staff that turned into a serpent, and, most memorably, the parting of the Red Sea just as the Israelites began to believe hope was lost. God did not give Moses the clear blueprint of what would happen over the course of the Exodus. Instead, Moses had to follow God step by step, trusting that God knew what He was doing. The tools that God gave to Moses got greater as the faith within Moses developed. Moses believed and acted. He surrendered to God's plan and served God. In the story of Moses and Exodus, we see two parallel reversals: Moses rises up from a position of lowliness, and the pharaoh is cast down from his high position. Moses initially believed that he was not good enough to do the work God had called him to do but chose to trust God rather than to dwell on his personal unworthiness. Moses focused not on rising to greatness or achieving glory but on serving God and freeing God's people.

The story of Moses is not the only story in the Bible to

show how God's faithfulness brings about unexpected reversals. Look at Esther, the Hebrew slave girl who became the queen of Persia and then risked her life to stand and ask the king to save God's people. The Bible clarifies that Esther had to confront a profound fear and that she questioned whether God's path was really the best for her. Esther must have experienced great confusion at first when God put her into a high position and then required her to risk it all by approaching the king uninvited. Esther was reminded by Mordecai to trust God's plan. Mordecai pointed out that Esther might have become queen specifically "for such a time as this."

The life of King David provides us with another example of how God brings about such radical reversals. By man's view, David was a young, inexperienced shepherd boy. Those who observed David in his young life believed that he should certainly not be chosen to be king of Israel and that he should not be sent to kill Goliath. David's ability was questioned, but in God's view, he was perfect for the jobs he was called to do. Because David had faith and acted through God, he accomplished great deeds for God's kingdom.

We see it again with Joseph. Abandoned by his brothers and sold into slavery, he later became the second most powerful person in Egypt and saved Egypt and nearby countries from famine. We see it even more in the New Testament: Look at the disciples. By the world's standards, they were nobodies. But the disciples believed and followed, surrendering to God and serving Him. We see it again with the apostle Paul. Paul made a name for himself in the world by persecuting and killing

Christians. And yet God worked through Paul, whom we now remember as the most prominent writer of the New Testament.

All these people are remembered for the important deeds they were able to do for God. But before they acted, before they believed and followed, each one had to get past self-doubt. Before they could act, they had to overcome the belief that they were not good enough to do what they were called to do. They had to choose not to fear.

Such historical personages got past their self-doubt, past the junk that held them back, believed, and acted from faith in God. They showed their love for God by loving God's people. Every one of us has this opportunity to act, but we don't tell stories about the ones who choose not to act. These people who do not act on the opportunities God has given them let their fear of failure have greater control over their minds and hearts than the call of God has. They don't trust the creator of the universe. You see that God does not make us great. He gives us the option to choose greatness and then helps us every step of the way. Listening to God's direction in our lives leads us to the greatness that can be found in loving God and loving others.

Be intentional! Make the unequivocal decision to love God and to love others. If you do so, you will get past all the junk: the fear, the false beliefs, the "I'm not good enoughs" that this world has to offer. You can then begin to see all the possibilities God has to offer. You will begin to see the ideas and tools you need to harvest the seeds God has planted in you. You will truly find a godly kind of greatness. Even if the world does not recognize this unique kind of greatness, God does, and you will.

God, you have made the world with your word, your will, and your intention. You have created good things because you have intended to, and you have created me to live with a similar intentionality. Mold my will to yours so that, with the similar intentionality, I can direct my life to be lived for you and follow in your footsteps. Amen.

Day 9

Prayer

And so I tell you, keep on asking, and you will receive what you ask for. Keep on seeking, and you will find. Keep on knocking, and the door will be opened to you. For everyone who asks, receives. Everyone who seeks, finds. And to everyone who knocks, the door will be opened.

You fathers—if your children ask for a fish, do you give them a snake instead? Or if they ask for an egg, do you give them a scorpion? Of course not! So if you sinful people know how to give good gifts to your children, how much more will your heavenly Father give the Holy Spirit to those who ask him.

—Luke 11:9–13

Many people use prayer only as a to-do list for God. These prayers go somewhat along the lines of, "Dear Lord, here is my to-do list for today. Please get it all done by close of business. Amen." This attitude towards prayer fails to recognize the full truth that life with God is a relationship. A prayerful relationship with God is like all relationships. Its quality depends on what you put into it. We can see in earthly examples that a to-do list approach to communicating just doesn't work. Imagine a parent-child relationship in which the child got up every morning and gave the parent a to-do list for the day. Suppose that child then ignored the relationship until he or she encountered difficulties or faced danger or fear, then cried out to the parent for help. We can imagine the ridiculousness of that situation, and yet that is the relationship we cultivate when we have a similar attitude with God.

Parents know or should know what their children need. They also know that there is a difference between what they need and what they want. Most importantly, children need to learn. A child will learn by watching and listening, from circumstances, and from other experiences. We tend to try to grow our relationship with God through talking to Him, but we often forget that an integral part of a relationship with God is time listening to Him.

So how do we listen for God? There are five primary channels that God uses to speak to us. Through them, we must listen well to what God has to say to us. These channels are the following.

- the Bible
- our own thoughts
- the words and actions of others
- circumstances we encounter
- audible or otherwise direct communication

There are many examples of direct communication in the Bible, but most of us rarely or never experience it in the present time. Instead, most of us encounter God through the other four channels. God is speaking to us all the time, flooding us with communication, like the seeds the farmer sows in Jesus's parable. Usually we don't even realize the blessings of communication that God is pouring on us because we have not trained ourselves to be good listeners and observers of God's messages to us. If we focus on staying on God's path of salvation, doing our two jobs of surrender and service, and living a life without fear, these practices can allow us to become amazingly attuned to God's daily nudges.

Along with being able to listen for God, we must also learn discernment. We must be able to tell when messages come from God. This can be difficult, but there are three criteria that can help you to know if the message you are receiving is truly from God. You can be sure that it is God speaking to you if all three of these questions can be answered with a *yes*.

- Is what God telling you good?
- Is what God telling you consistent with what Jesus said in the Bible?
- Is what God telling you not about you, your self-glorification, ego, or desires but about how you can serve others?

God never wants you to do something evil. So if what you think God is telling you is something that is hurtful to others, that is not God. God does not tell His children to get angry, take revenge, or hurt others. God wants you to do good and consistently gives you opportunities to do good. When we listen to God, we hear the ways that God wants us to do good in the world—to bring God's perfect reality closer to our own present reality.

Second, to know what God is calling us to do, it is essential that we familiarize ourselves with the words of Jesus. A plain language Bible can help you build your knowledge of the words of Christ. An updated translation will make Christ's words more accessible, easier to remember. Read what Jesus has said again and again. Become familiar with His words so you have a reference to know if what you sense from God is consistent with what Jesus said. There are other places in the Bible to go to for wisdom and knowledge to illustrate further what Jesus meant when He spoke. John, Paul, Peter, and James wrote letters to the early believers to keep those early believers living on God's path. Those letters will keep you on His path as well. Theologians use the phrase "scripture interpreting scripture" to refer to the process of understanding what the Bible has to say through comparison to other scriptures. We can use Jesus's words as a baseline to see how we should understand the rest of the Bible and to form a greater understanding of how the Bible should impact our lives.

The third test for us to know if God is speaking to us is the toughest one to follow. Our human nature and even our survival instincts push us to think that everything should always be about us. Although there are certainly times when those instincts are needed, the Bible calls us to remember that the Christian life is ultimately not about ourselves but about having faith and acting to serve others.

Perhaps you are asking for God's wisdom to understand how to do what your Father wants you to do so you can achieve your full potential as His son or daughter. Imagine what happens if you choose to learn from God all that He wishes for you and to follow that path. What will you receive if you first seek Him?[59] You will receive the answer to the most basic prayer: "Help my life to get better." You see, God has set this all up in a counterintuitive way. To get our own true desires, we must first learn to be unselfish. When we seek God, our desires begin to align more closely with His own desires, and we find that God delights to grant our desires when we are following Him.[60]

When you pray, here is an outline you can follow. It will help you listen for God and align your desires with God's perfect desires.

First, praise God and give Him thanks for all that He has done and all that He is about to do with you.[61]

Second, ask how you can serve Him today. Go through your schedule with God and ask that He make it His, to guide and direct you through each event. You want God to be present in the classroom, the boardroom, the shop, the factory, the home, or on the air plane. Wherever you go, ask God to be there with you.

Third, ask God for His wisdom.[62] God promises that if you ask for His wisdom, He will give it to you. So take Him up on that promise. You may find that it is easier to receive

God's wisdom then to follow it, but know that all learning is incremental, no less in this case than in any other.

Finally, conclude your time of prayer by silently listening for God. Twenty minutes seems necessary to get to a deep level of consciousness and tune in deeply with what God has to say.

There are many resources for help in learning to listen prayerfully to God. One method that is particularly helpful is called "Centering Prayer." The Trappist monk, Thomas Keating, writes helpfully about to how to cultivate this practice of listening to God.[63]

An additional tool that may be helpful is *Jesus Calling* by Sarah Young. The book takes you through a daily journey of giving your fears and concerns to God, using Bible verses that are written in the first person, as if Jesus is speaking them to you directly. It makes a great addition to a daily devotional routine—it reminds us how God's calling has a direct hold on each of our lives.

Finally, pray for others. Pray for those you care about and also pray for your enemies.[64] Release to God whatever they are doing to harm you.[65] Let it go and forgive and pray for them in an earnest and loving way. Forgiveness is a gift you give yourself. Close your prayers by asking for God's favor, and ask it all in Jesus Christ's name.[66]

Father, as I continue to seek your face and learn to live in your authentic confidence rather than fear, draw me nearer to you. God, I pray that you will help me pray and listen for you with more trust and more faith. Guide me in the path of prayer as you guide me in all paths. Amen.

Love

Dear friends, let us continue to love one another, for love comes from God. Anyone who loves is a child of God and knows God. But anyone who does not love does not know God, for God is love.

All who declare that Jesus is the Son of God have God living in them, and they live in God. We know how much God loves us, and we have put our trust in his love.

God is love, and all who live in love live in God, and God lives in them. And as we live in God, our love grows more perfect. So we will not be afraid on the day of judgment, but we can face him with confidence because we live like Jesus here in this world.

Such love has no fear, because perfect love expels all fear. If we are afraid, it is for fear of punishment, and this shows that we have not fully experienced his perfect love. We love each other because he loved us first.

If someone says, "I love God," but hates a fellow believer, that person is a liar; for if we don't love people we can see how can we love God, whom we cannot see? And he has given us this command: Those who love God must also love their fellow believers.

—1 John 4:7, 15–21

It is easy to love the people whom we love but much harder to love those we dislike. Yet God commands that we must do both. When you do so, your brain will change, and you will begin to be transformed into a person of grace, compassion, friendship, and love. You will move toward being able to love others as God loves you. To be more like God is powerful. After all, God loves you unconditionally, even though He does not always like your conduct. He is there for you even when you reject Him and forgives you even before you accept Him back. Just as a good parent does with a child, God loves His children no matter what.[67] God's love is there even when one of His children rejects actions that would be good for them. Even when a child engages in self-destructive behavior, a good parent never wavers in parental love. A good parent rejoices when the lessons of self-destruction lead to transformation. God is a perfect parent. It is better to listen to Him first than to learn from your own self-destructive behavior.

So God teaches us to love one another. Pray for your enemies but also don't let your guard down against those who would seek to harm you. Operate in God's authentic love, and your heart and mind will change at a deep level. You will be freed from the fear-based thoughts that occupy your brain and keep you from achieving your fullest God-given potential. Jesus instructs those who follow Him to do unto others as they would prefer others to do unto them.[68] If you do this faithfully and choose to love others and act lovingly toward them, you will find that the more you love others, the greater your capacity for love will be. The more you cultivate your capacity for love, the more fear, insecurity, anger, resentment, and pain die and are permanently replaced with that love.

Write a list of ways you can present yourself differently to the people around you by always acting through love first. Start with the people in your life whom you love, then work your way to the people who irritate you, and then to the ones you don't like. Not only can this process change you—it has the amazing potential to transform those around you in a miraculous way.

Holy God, your transformative love is holding the universe together. Your love is bringing your kingdom into our present reality. And your love is transforming me from the inside out, allowing me to become fearless and to live fearlessly in your coming kingdom. Lord, with your love so powerful and transforming, transform me into one who loves powerfully. Let my love for you and for others make me fearless and equip me to bring your kingdom fearlessly a little closer to my everyday reality. Amen.

Day 11

Forgiveness

Then Peter came to him and asked, "Lord, how often should I forgive someone who sins against me? Seven times?"

"No, not seven times," Jesus replied, "but seventy times seven!

"Therefore, the Kingdom of Heaven can be compared to a king who decided to bring his accounts up to date with servants who had borrowed money from him. In the process, one of his debtors was brought in who owed him millions of dollars. He couldn't pay, so his master ordered that he be sold—along with his wife, his children, and everything he owned—to pay the debt.

"But the man fell down before his master and begged him, 'Please, be patient with me, and I will pay it all.' Then his master was filled with pity for him, and he released him and forgave his debt.

"But when the man left the king, he went to a fellow servant who owed him a few thousand dollars. He grabbed him by the throat and demanded instant payment.

"His fellow servant fell down before him and begged for a little more time. 'Be patient with me, and I will pay it,' he pleaded. But his creditor wouldn't wait. He had the man arrested and put in prison until the debt could be paid in full.

"When some of the other servants saw this, they were very upset. They went to the king and told him everything that had happened. Then the king called in the man he had forgiven and said, 'You evil servant! I forgave you that tremendous debt because you pleaded with me. Shouldn't you have mercy on your fellow servant, just as I had mercy on you?' Then the angry king sent the man to prison to be tortured until he had paid his entire debt.

"That's what my heavenly Father will do to you if you refuse to forgive your brothers and sisters from your heart."

—Matthew 18:21–35

Scientific studies have found that anger, resentment, and revenge reside in the frontal lobes of the brain, but they are not the only emotions that the frontal lobes generate. These lobes are also the most creative parts of the brain.[69] If those billions of synapses in your brain are busy figuring out how to get even with those who have harmed you, then the most creative part of your brain is occupied with self-destructive thoughts. The synaptic nerves seek more synaptic nerves to dedicate to anger, resentment, and revenge, which ultimately damages your creative ability.[70] That is why forgiveness is the gift you give yourself. In the New Testament, the Greek word *aphiemi* means *forgiveness*, but it can also mean *release*. In other words, to forgive is to release, to let it go.[71] Forgiving someone is often of little benefit to that person, but for the person who forgives, a powerful event happens to billions of synaptic nerves in the brain. Those nerves that occupy the most creative part of the brain now become free to do creative work for good rather than evil. People who offer forgiveness become free to create solutions to problems, to build relationships, and to achieve amazing success. This is all because they are no longer focused on hurt, pain, anger, resentment, and revenge.

It is not easy to let the offense go when someone has hurt us. In most cases, society does not expect us to forgive. The more terrible the betrayal or the actions of others, the more we are expected to seek revenge rather than forgiveness. Do not mistake the call to forgiveness with a lack of consequences. The sinner will face consequences for the sin,[72] but these consequences will not come from you. Forgiveness is not meant to benefit the offender but is for your benefit.[73] God has given us this tool to free the most creative part of the brain. Every day someone does something directly or indirectly to hurt you or the ones you love. It might be as little as gossip or as big as stealing from you. For the little offenses, there is little to do but let them go! For crimes against you, still call the police and give testimony of the crime. Let the criminal face the consequences. But in your own heart, in your mind, let it go! A state of unforgiveness imprisons not only the criminal but also yourself. When you forgive, the prisoner you truly release is you.[74]

You can see that each of these tools is tougher than the one before. That is where God is indispensable once again. Always trying to forgive on your own is nearly impossible, but when you have God acting as a perfect third party in your interactions with others, it becomes much easier. God, who loves you, is that perfect third party. God is ready to take your sin and relieve you of its burden. When you pray, forgive all who have hurt you or seek to hurt you and give that pain and hurt to Christ. Exchange your pain for His love. Take His yoke upon you, for His burden is light.[75]

Write down the top three evil things that someone else has done to you and release that list to God in prayer. Pray to the Lord and forgive that person from the heart. Don't tell the other person that you have forgiven them unless they ask for your forgiveness. This process is one that restores you and allows you to let go of your own bitterness. It is not about the other person.

Father, I have not deserved your forgiveness, and yet you

have given it to me freely, out of your deep love and concern for me. For this I thank you, and I pray that as I learn to rest fearlessly in the reality of your forgiveness, you will equip me to forgive others fearlessly as well. Forgiveness is a bold act that must be done out of love. It cannot be done from fear. God, I pray that you will give me the boldness to dare to forgive others, even my enemies. Amen.

Day 12

Gratitude

Always be full of joy in the Lord. I say it again—rejoice! Let everyone see that you are considerate in all you do. Remember, the Lord is coming soon.

Don't worry about anything; instead, pray about everything. Tell God what you need, and thank him for all he has done. Then you will experience God's peace, which exceeds anything we can understand. His peace will guard your hearts and minds as you live in Christ Jesus.

—Philippians 4:4–7

How often do you pray for miracles and miss the miracles that are all around you? As C. S. Lewis wrote, "Prayer does not change God; it changes you." Prayer begins to change your perspective by physically changing your brain. Prayer gradually and miraculously brings you into relationship with God so that you can live your life on His path and with His timing, which benefits you and those around you. It's true that when you pray for miracles, they sometimes happen just as you request them, but we also confront the reality that sometimes miracles don't happen when we pray for them. This is because God always sees the bigger picture. God can see every molecule in the whole universe. He invented time for us.[76] Time does not limit God. No matter how we screw things up, God still uses our sin and imperfection in a perfect and good way that surpasses our own understanding.[77] We may never know why a disappointment occurred, and we may never know how that disappointment was used to accomplish God's greater good. What happens today has impact that echoes thousands and even millions of years from now.[78] How you raise your children, treat your spouse, or even interact with strangers will have impacts that can ripple out for generations. *It's a Wonderful Life*[79] demonstrates, through a compelling story, how one person's life can have an effect on so many others. Even the little deeds we do without thinking can set in motion a chain of events that cause great or terrible events to happen. While the movie is fiction, the message is reality. God can track all this action and He can allow events to happen or regulate them when it is necessary. God does this in a way that surpasses our ability to understand.

Here is the main point: If you ask God for a miracle, it may happen, but if you are living by His path, you will see the miraculous in the everyday.[80] When you seek to grow in faith and become that fertile soil, you will not only reap the benefits of God's kingdom, you will gain a perspective that allows you to see His miracles every day.

Mark Batterson, in *The Grave Robber,* uses the illustration of Jesus's miracles to point out that God's miracles are all around us, but we usually take them for granted or fail to see them. Just think that in the last twenty-four hours, you traveled 1.5 million miles through space at a speed of sixty-seven thousand miles per hour, on a ball spinning at a thousand miles per hour, and you did not even notice.[81] Welcome to miracles you take for granted. If that daily miracle were one degree off either way, we would burn or freeze to death.

Look at the Translational Genomics Project.[82] This genomics project was launched by a group of scientists in 2002. Their goal was first to map the human genome, then to map other animal and plant genomes. The scientists discovered that, on a genomic level, all humans are 99.5 percent identical. Dr. Jeffery Trent, world-renowned scientist and founder of the Translational Genomics Institute, points to the project as evidence of intelligent design.[83] Trent points out that every gene in any human is 99.5 percent the same as those of everyone else. That means that less than one half of 1 percent of you is unique. That .5 percent determines all the traits that make you different from other human beings. We think of ourselves as completely unique from one another, but we are almost all the same—all made in the image of our creator. Surprisingly, we are even gnomically very similar to every living thing on Earth. For instance, your genetics are only 25 percent different from those of a mouse. Yet we can see that 25 percent makes a remarkable difference.[84]

Start seeing these everyday miracles; recognize what is all around you as a miracle. Everything is a miracle. The fact that you were ever born is miraculous—think about the millions of years of events that had to break right for you to exist. God does the miraculous work of sustaining creation every day because He loves you. Trust in Him who made you and is doing miracles for you every day. Change your perspective. Do your two jobs: Surrender to His will for you, accept Christ and His Holy Spirit, and fear not! God loves us! It is up to us to live that life of God's love by changing our perspective and loving others!

Forgiveness is tough, but even tougher is the call to be grateful in all matters, even the crappy ones.[85] Ultimately, though, the result of gratitude is happiness. Happiness is a decision you make. Let's start by examining the part of gratitude that seems easy. Can you go through a day identifying every good event that happens to you on that day and thank God for it gratefully? We discover, upon trying this, that it is actually nearly impossible to count your blessings—they are so abundant that we tend to take so many of them for granted. When you take blessings for granted, you don't value the blessing, which means that you don't feel blessed. Instead you just see the challenges of your day and become depressed, insecure, or fearful.

Let's start with a few basic truths. You are fully and unconditionally loved by God.[86] He loves you so much that He showed His love through His life, death, and resurrection.[87] He gave you life so that you may give life to others. And there is even more. We are surrounded by small, daily miracles, which we often don't see. Look at the grocery store, for instance. If someone who lived eighteenth century were to go into one, that person would be amazed. Think about how much goes into growing, delivering, and displaying the food on the shelves. So many conditions have to be just right for the food to grow, and so much infrastructure has to be in place for the food to end up on store shelves. Walking into a grocery store is a small, everyday miracle. And yet we so often take it for granted. We do not think to give thanks when we walk into a grocery store because it has become such a typical part of our experience. There are also all the precious things we know we should be grateful for but too often take for granted: the ones we love and the ones who love us. You will find that if you can go through your day giving thanks for all the amazing miracles that surround you, your perspective will change. In fact, your brain will literally change: The synapses that are connected around curmudgeonly feelings will start disconnecting and reconnect around thoughts of appreciation, internal peace, and joy.[88] All this comes through gratitude.

Start recognizing all the good things in your life. Take a moment, pause, and be grateful. Begin being grateful even for events that don't work out the way you want. Begin anticipating that good can and will come from the disappointing events. Before you know it, even "...your biggest disappointments will turn into your best opportunities".[89] Finally, be grateful even for the tragedies in your life. This kind of gratitude is the hardest to come by, and it comes by finding the joy in all you had before you lost it or the goodness that will come when the evil is finally overcome. This attitude absolutely requires help from God. We must remember that God does not create tragedy. God gives humans free will. The results of our free will have consequences, which is why we see evil in the world. The results of such evil often may extend beyond the immediate action and last for multiple generations. The consequences of the choices that some make may be devastating to many. This devastation is the price of free will. God gives all of us the path to Him, but all of us fall short, and sometimes the results of such shortcomings can be devastating. The world is populated with imperfect people, so our free will comes at a price. God would rather give us free will than control our every action because He wants us to choose Him freely. God wants what a perfect father would want of any child.

The good news is that God takes our disastrous decisions and always turns them to good, sometimes in ways we won't even understand at the time. The good results always happen, even if we are not around to see the good that comes. And we know that in all things, God works for the good of those who love Him, who have been called according to His purpose.[90] What man means for evil, God will use for good.[91] So even in the midst of tragedy, we are called to make an effort to be grateful for the good that can come from the tragedy and all the gifts that came before it. In doing so, God will help you recover more quickly from the pain of the tragedy. He will reveal the glory of the moment in His time. He may even reveal it to you sooner if you ask.

Remember to consider it pure joy when you face various troubles. Ask God for His wisdom and He will give it to you.[92] Remember to be grateful in all ways.

God, this world you have created is deeply beautiful—from the nature that surrounds us to the love within and between our hearts, you have made creation good. For these things, my thanks is not enough, but it is what I have to offer. Lead me to revel in the intricate beauty of everything in the world you have created and that you sustain and uphold. Draw me to the emotion of gratitude again and again. Let me always rest in the knowledge of how graciously you have provided for me by your love. Amen.

Day 13

Ministry in Disguise

And so, dear brothers and sisters, I plead with you to give your bodies to God because of all he has done for you. Let them be a living and holy sacrifice—the kind he will find acceptable. This is truly the way to worship him. Don't copy the behavior and customs of this world, but let God transform you into a new person by changing the way you think. Then you will learn to know God's will for you, which is good and pleasing and perfect.

—Romans 12:1–2

Most of us do not think of ourselves as ministers, but we are all ministers in one way or another. We are called to send out messages every day by word and conduct. A quote frequently attributed to St Francis says to "preach often, and when necessary use words."[93] Everything you do is a ministry—either for good or for selfishness. While the opposite of love is fear it may also be selfishness.[94] Make today the day you start thinking about everything you do as a ministry, even if that ministry is disguised as something else.

Your work or your business, for instance, could be a ministry. In *God Owns My Business*,[95] Stanley Tamm writes about his experience of giving his business to God and beginning to run the business as "God's Trustee." Because Tamm was able to do this, the business not only succeeded; it also had a transformative power on the lives of those with whom Tamm interacted. Although he did not work in a church, Tamm was a minister. His tool and dye company became a kind of church for him to witness to God's power of transformation. But you don't have to own the company to be a minister in one. No matter what your job is, you can wake up every day with the attitude that you are going to give the day and your job to God. Do your very best and care about others even if they do not care about you. God will lead you every day to ministry moments: opportunities to witness to others the grace and love of Christ through your actions and words. I believe that Christ gives us the perfect business plan for business and life. How to grow your business, treat your customers and competitors, and resolve disputes are issues all perfectly addressed by Jesus. Christ's principles work every time and in every setting.

Disguised ministry goes even beyond the workplace, however. Ministry can be performed as a parent or a spouse, a sibling, or a friend. In these relationships, you can minister not by preaching but by teaching through your examples of love, encouragement, service, and commitment to your relational life.

Whether at work or at play, at home or away, you have opportunities for disguised ministry. The tools of your ministry are these tools we have already discussed: the words of Jesus, a love for God and others, service to others, prayer, and attentive listening.

Live your life. Make it a ministry. Take the time each day to pray through your schedule for that day. Pray for each event or meeting and ask God to arrange your day to have maximum impact for Him. Pray and ask that each meeting will accomplish its intended task and also that God will use these relational encounters to do more. Then listen for the Holy Spirit's promptings throughout your day. You will be amazed at how each day will become an adventure in ministry.

Gracious God, you have placed me exactly where you intend me to be—my life, my friends, my work, and my family all offer the opportunities for ministry that you have provided for me. Go before me, God, and show me how I can live faithfully in your calling in the ministry context in which you have already placed me. Give me the energy and joy to live in witness to your love, daring to have a transformative effect on the world around me. Protect me, Lord, from feeling discouraged when I don't see obvious results and from feeling despair when this ministry gets difficult. Empower me, today and every day, to live the beautiful ministry opportunities you have given to me.

Day 14

Putting It All Together

Immediately after this, Jesus insisted that his disciples get back into the boat and cross to the other side of the lake, while he sent the people home. After sending them home, he went up into the hills by himself to pray. Night fell while he was there alone.

Meanwhile, the disciples were in trouble far away from land, for a strong wind had risen, and they were fighting heavy waves. About three o'clock in the morning Jesus came toward them, walking on the water. When the disciples saw him walking on the water, they were terrified. In their fear, they cried out, "It's a ghost!"

But Jesus spoke to them at once. "Don't be afraid," he said. "Take courage. I am here!"

Then Peter called to him, "Lord, if it's really you, tell me to come to you, walking on the water."

"Yes, come," Jesus said.

So Peter went over the side of the boat and walked on the water toward Jesus. But when he saw the strong wind and the waves, he was terrified and began to sink. "Save me, Lord!" he shouted.

Jesus immediately reached out and grabbed him. "You have so little faith," Jesus said. "Why did you doubt me?"

When they climbed back into the boat, the wind stopped. Then the disciples worshiped him. "You really are the Son of God!" they exclaimed.

—Matthew 14:22–33

Peter had the power to walk on water, just as Jesus had done, until he realized he was standing on the Sea of Galilee and became afraid. Peter's fear caused him to sink.

Fear causes all of us to sink or fall short of our authentic selves. If we do not address our subconscious fear, we are destined to let it run our lives—and to ruin them. If we do as most do and satisfy ourselves with merely working around our fears, we can manage to live an above-normal life. But what if you stopped running from your unconscious fears? What if you identified them, faced them, and properly called these fears what they are: lies? What if you used all the tools God has given you to eliminate those subconscious lies, those fears that enslave you?

What would be the scope of your potential if your whole brain was free of its fears—free to create, grow, innovate, and love just as God designed us to do?

If we humans can trust in the promises of God that come from salvation, love God and others, surrender to God, and serve those around us, then we could realize a life of joy, free of fear!

This is the life we are offered—a life full of beautiful and unbelievable possibility, a life that sees and acknowledges all the miracles around us, a life of participating in those miracles by serving others, a healthier, happier, and freer life.

Remember that once the disciples walked in total faith after witnessing Christ transformed after believing fully and leaving doubt and fear behind. They, too, were able to do all the miracles that Jesus did while he was on earth.

These miracles are possible, but they start with changing your mind—identifying the controlling fears and lies, marking them as lies, and repeating the truth three times. Every time those lies rear their ugly heads, respond by calling them lies and replacing them with the truth. Give those fears to God and let them go. Give anger, hurt, resentment, and revenge over to God and let them go. Free yourself of the captive life that fear induces. Give these burdens to God and live in joy. Live in God's authentic confidence.

John Kaites

Dear Lord,

It is a lie that I must fear anything. I give my fear to you. The truth is that you want me to live in your authentic love. I have accepted Christ as my Lord and Savior. I see the world through the lens of loving you and loving others. I surrender all that I have and declare it yours. I shall act as your trustee. So, Lord, give me your wisdom. Take my fear away. Help my trust for you grow and give me your favor as I give my favor in service to others. In Jesus Christ's holy name, amen.

Author Notes

In the winter of 2013, while I was sitting in church, an outline for this book downloaded itself into my head. When I went home, I wrote the outline down on the back of an envelope and spent the next few months struggling to understand why God had called me to write a book of any kind, let alone this book. Nearly every day I would seek God's guidance on the words He wanted me to write. As I sought friends with experience in writing, they recommended various formulas for writing a successful book. The most common was to write my life's story as the hook that interests readers in the subject. I have no desire to write a book; I had no desire to go to seminary and become a pastor, and likewise no desire to read music and play the piano. None of these prospects interested me. Sports interest me. I am interested in influence, success, solving complex political and legal issues, fighting a good fight, creating businesses and wealth—seemingly all for the benefit of my family, if not the good of mankind. Through a series of growth moments in my life, my journey has steadily led to an increased dependence on the triune God and a desire to be constantly in relationship with Him. To that end, it was like the stock market—my relationship with God grew over time, but some days were up and others down. Not happy or sad up and down but more like sinner verses saint up and down. Sometimes I felt so connected to God that I could physically feel the Holy Spirit, and other times I felt clawed back to the normal, yet sinful, ways of this world. Yet the net effect was a closer relationship with the Father over time.

I pray throughout my day, giving praise and thanks for this life and the miracles that are all around me. I ask God for His wisdom and favor. I ask God for good things and also, sometimes, for things that aren't so good for me, knowing that I do not need to have any fear or shame about the flawed person that I am. I figure God made me and already knows my defective parts. As time went by, I would consistently ask God what He wanted me to do with this epiphany book outline. I struggled with a number of drafts, writing about my life and trying to make this the book that I had been told would be interesting and likely to succeed. Then, one morning at 3 a.m., in August of 2014, I woke up. As I was praying and praising God, these powerful thoughts came to my head: This book is not about me. I felt that I should refrain from the temptation to make the book about me and my own experience and instead focus on God and on what is true about God for everyone. I should just write it as it was given to me. So, through a stream of consciousness, I went to the computer and began to write. In one short week, the first draft of this text was written. The words poured out of me like water—pouring through my fingertips and onto the page.

At the end of that week, I marveled at what God had done. Through me, God had created a full manuscript, and I had the earnest hope that God would use this text to change lives. At first blush, the text did not always flow smoothly, and I was not sure I could completely annotate or prove all that I had written. So I set a course to footnote all that had been written. I attempted to clean up the grammar and syntax without changing the impact of the thoughts. I found authority for most of the text and decided to use endnotes for the readers to explore each concept more deeply if they wish. The heart of the message that God wants you to hear is this.

Fear not and trust God. Seek God, who is pure love, at every possible moment, and your life will be transformed. You will begin to live a life without fear and anxiety, a life of connection to the Father and His pure love. He wants us all to choose that path.

The 14 Daily Prayers

Day 1

God, we thank you because you call us to follow fearlessly, surrendering to your perfect plan. Today and through the rest of my life, help me follow the simple but difficult practice of living fearlessly. Lord, give me your wisdom and favor. I pray that you be with me as I follow you fearlessly into the beautiful promises you have for me and for my role in your creation. Amen.

Day 2

Lord God, thank you for making our minds in such a way that, through your help, we can become fearless. Help me enter into this day and every day with a little more trust in you and a little less fear. Help me to live not from fear but from faith. Thank you for being my God, for watching over my life so I do not need to fear. Amen.

Day 3

Lord Jesus, thank you for loving me unconditionally. I love you back and accept you as my personal Lord and Savior. Forgive me for my sin and become the Lord of my life. In your name I pray. Amen.

Day 4

Father God, you have created me and drawn me toward you into your perfect love. You have set before me specific tasks so that I can be your hands and feet, living in the world to shine your light. Work in me and be with me so that I can live in my calling, which you have placed on me. Show me the places in my life where I can increase in love and grant me the power to do so. God, be with your people and help us to love you and to love others well. Increase your love in us every day so that we may shine brightly in witness to you. Amen.

Day 5

I love you, God. I surrender to you my life. I give all that I have to you for your purpose because I trust you above all else. I am the trustee of all that you have given me. Give me your wisdom and tell me what you want me to do, and I will do it. Give me the faith and the tools to make the improbable probable and the impossible possible because you are my Lord, my Savior and my king.

Day 6

Lord God, I come to you aware of how much love you have expressed for me—in the creation of the world, in beauty I witness in everyday life, and in your sacrifice for my sins on the cross. I pray, Lord, that you will draw me into a life where I can love and serve others from a place of gratitude for the way you have loved and served me. Help me to see today how I can operate from love in the decisions I make today.

Day 7

Lord, thank you for showing your radical love for me—in the creation of the world, in the cross of Christ, and in the way you sustain and uphold my life every single day. Father, I pray that as you continue to show your love for me, I will begin to rest more firmly in the knowledge and assurance of your love. I pray that resting in your love will allow me to become fearless—and to live fearlessly a life wholly devoted to you. Amen.

Day 8

God, you have made the world with your word, your will, and your intention. You have created good things because you have intended to, and you have created me to live with a similar intentionality. Mold my will to yours so that, with the similar intentionality, I can direct my life to be lived for you and follow in your footsteps. Amen.

Day 9

Father, as I continue to seek your face and learn to live in your authentic confidence rather than fear, draw me nearer to you. God, I pray that you will help me pray and listen for you with more trust and more faith. Guide me in the path of prayer as you guide me in all paths. Amen.

Day 10

Holy God, your transformative love is holding the universe together. Your love is bringing your kingdom into our present reality. And your love is transforming me from the inside out, allowing me to become fearless and to live fearlessly in your coming kingdom. Lord, with your love so powerful and transforming, transform me into one who loves powerfully. Let my love for you and for others make me fearless and equip me to bring your kingdom fearlessly a little closer to my everyday reality. Amen.

Day 11

Father, I have not deserved your forgiveness, and yet you have given it to me freely, out of your deep love and concern for me. For this I thank you, and I pray that as I learn to rest fearlessly in the reality of your forgiveness, you will equip me to forgive others fearlessly as well. Forgiveness is a bold act that must be done out of love. It cannot be done from fear. God, I pray that you will give me the boldness to dare to forgive others, even my enemies. Amen.

Day 12

God, this world you have created is deeply beautiful—from the nature that surrounds us to the love within and between our hearts, you have made creation good. For these things, my thanks is not enough, but it is what I have to offer. Lead me to revel in the intricate beauty of everything in the world you have created and that you sustain and uphold. Draw me to the emotion of gratitude again and again. Let me always rest in the knowledge of how graciously you have provided for me by your love. Amen.

Day 13

Gracious God, you have placed me exactly where you intend me to be—my life, my friends, my work, and my family all offer the opportunities for ministry that you have provided for me. Go before me, God, and show me how I can live faithfully in your calling in the ministry context in which you have already placed me. Give me the energy and joy to live in witness to your love, daring to have a transformative effect on the world around me. Protect me, Lord, from feeling discouraged when I don't see obvious results and from feeling despair when this ministry gets difficult. Empower me, today and every day, to live the beautiful ministry opportunities you have given to me.

Day 14

Dear Lord,

It is a lie that I must fear anything. I give my fear to you. The truth is that you want me to live in your authentic love. I have accepted Christ as my Lord and Savior. I see the world through the lens of loving you and loving others. I surrender all that I have and declare it yours. I shall act as your trustee. So, Lord, give me your wisdom. Take my fear away. Help my trust for you grow and give me your favor as I give my favor in service to others. In Jesus Christ's holy name, amen!

Endnotes

1. ""Only Thing We Have to Fear Is Fear Itself": FDR's First Inaugural Address." *"Only Thing We Have to Fear Is Fear Itself": FDR's First Inaugural Address.* http://historymatters.gmu.edu/d/5057/.

2. Susan Q. Stranahan, "The Eastland Disaster Killed More Passengers Than the Titanic and the Lusitania. Why Has It Been Forgotten?" *Smithsonian.com.* October 27, 2014. http://www.smithsonianmag.com/history/eastland-disaster-killed-more-passengers-titanic-and-lusitania-why-has-it-been-forgotten-180953146/?no-ist.

3. James Ball, "September 11's indirect toll: road deaths linked to fearful flyers." *9/11: the 10th anniversary.* September 05, 2011, https://www.theguardian.com/world/2011/sep/05/september-11-road-deaths.

4. Gerhard Kittel, *Theological Dictionary of the New Testament Vol. IX:* - Edited by Gerhard Friedrich. (Eerdmans Publishing Company, 1974), 364-370; Darryl Delhousaye, Phoenix Seminary, March 27, 2015.

5. Lloyd Ogilvie, *Facing the Future Without Fear: Prescriptions for Courageous Living in the New Millennium.* (Ann Arbor, MI: Vine Books, 2002).

6. Michael Rugnetta, "Neuroplasticity." *Encyclopedia Britannica,* February 5, 2014, https://www.britannica.com/science/neuroplasticity.

7. Mark Batterson, *The Grave Robber: How Jesus Can Make Your Impossible Possible.* (Grand Rapids, MI: Baker Publishing Group, 2015), 20.

8. Cleve Stevens, *The Best in Us: People, Profit, and the Remaking of Modern Leadership.* (New York: Beaufort Books, 2012), 70.

9. Craig Freudenrich, "How Nerves Work." *HowStuffWorks.* October 19, 2007. Accessed December 19, 2015, http://health.howstuffworks.com/human-body/systems/nervous-system/nerve.htm.

10. "Neurons & Synapses - Memory & the Brain - The Human Memory." *Neurons & Synapses - Memory & the Brain - The Human Memory.* http://www.human-memory.net/brain_neurons.html.

11. Stevens.

12. Stevens.

13. Rugnetta, 1.

14. Barbara Arrowsmith-Young, *The Woman Who Changed Her Brain: How I Left My Learning Disability Behind and Other Stories of Cognitive Transformation.* (New York: Simon & Schuster Paperbacks, 2013).

15. Andrew Newberg, and Mark Robert Waldman, *How God Changes Your Brain: Breakthrough Findings from a Leading Neuroscientist.* (New York: Ballantine Books Trade Paperbacks, 2010).

16. Stevens.

17. Stevens.

18. John 3:16, John 3:36, John 10:9, John 14:6. (New Living Translation)

19. John 14:6

20. Acts 4:12, 1 Timothy 2:5, John 8:24, John10:9.

21. Romans 5:8

22. 1 John 4:4

23. John 14:6

24. F.L. Booth, "The New Testament Miracles of Jesus" Bible Class Teaching Curriculum, Zion, IL 60099.

25. Grant R. Jeffrey, *The Signature of God.* (Tennessee: World Pub. Inc., 1998), 254-257.

26. Deuteronomy 6:5, Leviticus 19:18, Luke 10:27, Matthew 22:37, Mark 12:30–31, 1 John 4:7, 1 John 4:8, 1 John 4:21, Romans 13:8–9, Galatians 5:14.

27. Matthew 22:36–40

28. Deuteronomy 6:5

29. Leviticus 19:18

30. John 3:16

31. Romans 5:8

32. Matthew 5:44

33. Matthew 7:1

34. James 2:17

35. Genesis 1:1

36. Romans 8:28

37. Jeremiah 29:11, Luke 12:6–7.

38. Luke 6:27–36

39. Mark 4:2–9, Matthew 13:3–9, Mark 4:2–9, Luke 8:4–8, Matthew 13:18–23, Mark 4:13–20, and Luke 8:11–15.

40. Luke 6:37–38

41. Glenn Stanton, "What St. Francis of Assisi Didn't Actually Say." *National Catholic Register*. http://www.ncregister.com/blog/gstanton/what-st.-francis-of-assisi-didnt-actually-say.

42. Elisabeth Kubler-Ross, "When You Don't Choose Love You Choose Fear." *Awakin.org*. January 18, 2010. http://www.awakin.org/read/view.php?tid=680.

43. Stevens.

44. 1 John 4:16–21

45. Luke 12:22, Luke 12:25-26.

46. Stevens, 202–205.

47. Stevens, 30–43.

48. Adam Sicinski, "Practical and Actionable Ideas to Help You Overcome Your Fears." *IQ Matrix Blog*. December 30, 2016. http://blog.iqmatrix.com/overcome-your-fears.

49. Sicinski.

50. 2 Timothy 1:7

51. John 14:6

52. Philippians 4:13

53. Stevens, 174–178.

54. 2 Corinthians 5:7

55. Stevens, 30.

56. Mark 5:36

57. 1 Corinthians 1:27–29

58. Exodus 4:10–14

59. Matthew 6:33

60. Mark 10:44

61. Matthew 15:36-38

62. James 1:2–7

63. Thomas Keating, *Open Mind Open Heart*. (New York, NY.: The Continuum Publishing Co., 1991).

64. Matthew 5:54

65. Proverbs 16:7

66. John 14:14

67. Luke 15:11–32

68. Matthew 7:12, Luke 6:31.

69. Megan Feldman Bettencourt, "The Science of Forgiveness." *The Science of Forgiveness: "When You Don't Forgive You Release All the Chemicals of the Stress Response.* March 25, 2016. http://meganfeldman.com/the-science-of-forgiveness-when-you-dont-forgive-you-release-all-the-chemicals-of-the-stress-response/.

70. Harvey Lodish, "Neurotransmitters, Synapses, and Impulse Transmission." *Molecular Cell Biology.* 4th edition. January 01, 1970. https://www.ncbi.nlm.nih.gov/books/NBK21521/.

71. Gary Kinnaman, *The Beginner's Guide to Worshiping God*. (Gospel Light Publications, 2013), 92.

72. Galatians 6:7–8

73. Steve Hartman, "Love Thy Neighbor: Son's Killer Moves Next Door." *CBS News.* June 08, 2011. http://www.cbsnews.com/news/love-thy-neighbor-sons-killer-moves-next-door/.

74. Matthew West, Into the light. Sparrow Records B001878400, 2013, compact disc.

75. Matthew 11:28–30

76. 2 Peter 3:8–9

77. Proverbs 3:5, Philippians 4:7.

78. Genesis 16–21

79. *It's a Wonderful Life*. Directed by Frank Capra.

80. Batterson.

81. Batterson.

82. Jeffery Trent, "TGen History." *TGen History*, https://www.tgen.org/home/about/tgen-history.aspx#.VYwX143bKM8.

83. Jeffery Trent, personal email to the author, December 30, 2015.

84. Psalm 139:13-15

85. 1 Thessalonians 5:18

86. Romans 8:28–30, 1 Corinthians 13.

87. John 3:16–17

88. Jessica Stillman, "Gratitude Physically Changes Your Brain, New Study Says." *Inc.com*. January 15, 2016. http://www.inc.com/jessica-stillman/the-amazing-way-gratitude-rewires-your-brain-for-happiness.html.

89. Jerry Reinsdorf, personal conversation with the author, September 8, 1998.

90. Romans 8:28

91. Genesis 50:20

92. James 1:2–7

93. Stanton

94. Jacob Roebuck, "Loving Lynda (2016)." *Loving Lynda*. http://www.imdb.com/title/tt4997998/.

95. Stanley Tam, and Ken Anderson. *God Owns My Business*. (Camp Hill, PA: WingSpread Publishers, 2013).

About the Author

John Kaites is an American Entrepreneur, who has founded many successful businesses based on principles found in this book. He began his career as a broadcaster at the age of 16, became an attorney at age 25, a state representative at age 29, a state senator at age 31. He lost his election for state attorney general at age 34, then started a law firm that spun off a lobbying firm and 3 other companies. His faith evolved from the time he accepted Christ as his personal savior in 5th grade and continues to this day. At age 42 he attended Fuller Theological Seminary where he started on a path of personal transformation that continues. The principles he learned while attending seminary, how to pray and listen for God, pastoral care, intentionality and biblical truth became the foundation that transformation. He began taking the words of Christ in the gospels and the book of Acts and turning them into secular business principles. This led to an exponential growth in financial wealth. In 2013 he owned some or all of 18 companies and was a partner in a law firm of 40 lawyers. He since sold, or merged all but 9 of those companies and is Of Counsel to a law firm with over 260 lawyers. His current ministry is not only in business but he helps pastors and churches think more entrepreneurial. He created a model for churches to bring people to faith in Christ using current culture and a model for increasing ministry revenue, outside of the collection plate. He is a visiting pastor who enjoys the opportunity to occasionally preach. He is a graduate of Alleghany College, Duquesne University School of Law and Fuller Theological Seminary. John may be reached at john.westbow@gmail.com

Printed in the United States
By Bookmasters